TIME RICH

PRACTICE

TIME RICH PRACTICE

A step-by-step guide to having the time you need, and the things you want, from a business you love

CLIFF HARVEY

Katoa Health Publishing

Copyright © Cliff Harvey 2015

All rights reserved.

Published by Katoa Health Publishing, a division of

CC Industries Ltd.

7 Ascension Place, Rosedale, Auckland 0632, New Zealand

Visit our Web site at www.KatoaHealth.com

ISBN 978-0-473-32022-5

First Edition

For my Dad. Thanks for teaching me more about business than any school ever could.

ACKNOWLEDGEMENTS

My biggest thanks for this, my fourth book, go to my Dad, Maurice Harvey, who has always instilled in me a love for the game of business. Secondly, to all the friends, colleagues and clients who encouraged me to write a book and create a mentoring system (Holistic Performance Nutrition™) to help other practitioners. Especially I'd like to acknowledge my friends and partners who have inspired and worked with me in health, strength and wellness (the list is long): Colin Walker, Joe McQuillan, Gemma Ross, Dave Fitzsimmons, Steve Rosenbaum, Will Garrick, Rob and Amber Holah, Jim Talo and Carmen Bott, Julien Emery, Paul and Leah Hemsworth, Josh Neumann, Jon-Erik Kawamoto, Sarah Jamieson, Harry Toor, Steve Angell and Carolina Dillen.

My mentors in business; all very different in their various approaches, but from whom I have learnt so very much: Ian Brooks, David Walden, Geoff Ashenden, Trevor Bolland, and my sister who showed me that the school of life could be well complemented by *actual* schooling! Who would have thought this highschool drop-out would become an academic and educator? And on that note; more recently a group of people who helped to reignite my passion for nutrition by proving that there is the potential for change in a sometimes stolid industry—my research colleagues Mikki Williden and Grant Schofield—I guess we're all old dogs learning new tricks now?

PROLOGUE

As practitioners we are in the enviable position of doing something we love. We have the opportunity to help people to become healthier, happier, fitter and stronger. We have the opportunity to facilitate a process of change in which people can begin to *live* in a way that is more congruent with their values and ethos and we can live a life congruent with ours. We help people to reach their highest levels of performance and, most importantly, help them to live closer to the highest potential and highest purpose and when we do this effectively we also live closer to ours.

Sometimes though, the business of what we love doing becomes so difficult to manage that we become burnt-out or we lose the valuable time and energy that we need in order to give our best to clients and patients, and to do other things (outside of our practice-work) that drive our passion and purpose.

This book is designed to help you to be more effective as a practitioner living your life of passion and purpose. More than just a book about business it is a book about finding your life-purpose and how to translate that into a labour of love that fills you up physically, emotionally, mentally, spiritually AND financially. It's time to take the plunge…

Now go forth and conquer.

HOW TO USE THIS BOOK

Time Rich Practice is a 'how to' guide to starting and maintaining a business in health practice that allows you the time, money and energy to optimally live your life of passion and purpose, and to help your clients and patients do the same. *Time Rich Practice* can be read as a book to inspire and motivate you in your business and practice life, but it also has actions to perform throughout the book to reinforce the messages and provide direct action to encourage rapid growth and development of your business. I highly recommend you complete all the actions, in order to get the most out of the book. I also encourage you to commit to doing the exercises at the end of each chapter and to put aside just a little time each day to put into practice the strategies herein that will save you time and help to make you financially secure.

Contents

INTRODUCTION

I have taught sports and clinical nutrition, business concepts and other courses at the tertiary level, and over many years in practice have mentored in some form or other, hundreds of nutritionists, coaches, trainers and other health practitioners. Over this time I have noticed a disturbing trend; that many of my students and colleagues in the industry simply don't last. They drop out of the industry to take up more stable jobs, or scratch out a relatively meagre existence doing what they love, but in the process end up burning out and becoming disillusioned due to the pressure and stress of 'running a business'.

I have over the years had my run-ins with burn-out too, along with business failures, partnerships and ventures gone wrong, and the difficulties of simply keeping one's head above water, both financially and in terms of time and energy. But thankfully through all of that I've been able to develop strategies to make life easier, and have developed tools and information that allow me to serve my clients and patients' needs, whilst also allowing the time and energy to live a vital life of health and happiness.

It's not as hard as you might think.

Turn the page…let us begin a journey of discovery.

CHAPTER ONE

Making a Start

Creating your dream practice from scratch

"THERE ARE ONLY TWO MISTAKES ONE CAN MAKE ALONG THE ROAD TO TRUTH; NOT GOING ALL THE WAY, AND NOT STARTING."
~ SIDDHARTHA GAUTAMA (BUDDHA)

Why do you want to be in practice?

While the answer may seem obvious, it is not until we ask ourselves this important question that we really get to grips with our purpose as practitioners and business people. In fact, a great idea for much of what we do in life and business is to start any project by asking ourselves 'why' we are doing it, and how this aligns with our core values and ethos.

My hope would be that in asking this question most readers would have more answers than simply 'Money'! Because let's face it, if you simply wanted to get rich there are easier ways to do it than to be a health and wellness practitioner! The financial rewards can be considerable though, and this is especially true if the core values of WHY you are in this business continue to drive your passion and purpose to make your unique health, fitness and wellness practice a sustainable one.

Asking the big WHY is a great way to determine what your most important intended outcomes are, and whether what you are doing is congruent with your values. This question provides an end-focussed framework for determining which projects and business ventures mesh with your values and ethos set.

If, for example, I asked myself why *I* have been in health and wellness practice for going on 17 years (at time of writing) my answers would be:

- To serve others
- To create a positive impact on health and wellness in society
- To help people to be healthier and happier
- To continue to learn and grow
- To create financial security for myself, my friends and my family.

You will see that the financial goal is certainly present, but is only as important as the other aspects of a life-in-balance that provide for the day-to-day enjoyment and satisfaction from doing what we love to do. In fact they are the reasons why we do what we do.

Action: Ask yourself the big WHY?

Take some time to brainstorm your *why*. Think not about 'what' you do in practice, but more importantly what you hope to achieve out of it, AND what you hope to give back to your clients and patients and to society and your community.

Tools:

Start with Why by Simon Sinek – www.startwithwhy.com

DETERMINING YOUR BUSINESS VALUES & ETHOS

What is most important to you and your business?

For your business to have direction you need to create goals that give you focus and direction, and for those goals to be effective for helping you to live your life of passion and purpose, they need to be congruent with your values and ethos.

This means that the goals you set must move you in a direction that is in line with how you want to be living, because if you don't set the *right* goals you may end up living in a manner that you are completely unhappy with.

Because we crave direction we often search for goals to chase, without asking whether they are the right goals. And the right goals are ones that are congruent with our life purpose.

Our deepest values encapsulate the way that we feel things should be, the way that we feel we should be, and the way we would most like to live our life of perfect passion and purpose. If we can define these deepest values in words, we help to create a framework that solidifies the concepts into more concrete material for our mind to work with. This exploration and awareness allows for a greater recognition of the things in our environment that will help to make our dreams a reality, and most importantly provides a 'razor' for how we should act, allowing us to make better, easier choices in business and in life.

Action: Is my life congruent with my values?

Ask yourself the following questions and write down your answers:

How do you fill your space? (E.g. At home, at work)

What words define the 'state' of your home environment?

What words define the 'state' of your work environment?

How do you spend your spare time?

How do you spend your work time?

On what activities do you spend most of your energy?

What do you spend most of your money on?

Excluding rent and food, what do you spend most money on?

On what do you feel you spend most of your energy?

In what area of your life do you feel you are most organised?

What do you spend most of your time thinking about?

What do you most dream about doing for a living?

What do you most dream about doing as a hobby?

What do you most dream about having?

What do you talk about most?

In what area of your life are you most passionate?

In what area of your life do you set most of your goals?

What inspires you most?

Who inspires you most?

Does my current life define or defy my values?

Look back and ask yourself if each answer is positive or negative.

- If positive put into column a
- If negative put into column b
- Go through each column 'a' answer one-by-one and look for a 'theme' that the answer alludes to.
- Go through your column b answers and find a positive theme in place of the negative that you have indicated that you would like to be true in your life instead. Match these answers to the themes below too.

Find the 5 most common themes. These form your value-set and should be considered whenever a challenge or opportunity arises—does it *fit* with my values?

YOUR PERFECT WORK-LIFE BALANCE

You've now defined your core values and have a clear idea about what themes you want to instill in your life. The next step is to imagine the absolute 'best-case scenario' for your work-life situation.

When we imagine what we really want to be true, we begin to promote the importance (on a conscious and subconscious level) of making this a reality, and we are able to notice any resistance to this happening.

This serves two functions:

1) We begin to subtly influence our brains to make the achievement of our goals a reality. We do this in several ways, one of the most important being that we begin to recognise things, places and people that we should be bringing into our lives in order to make our goals a reality. This in effect is the neuroscience behind the spiritual 'law of attraction'.

2) We are able to recognise the resistance and fear that we hold around our goals. Awareness allows us to become more mindful of the subconscious patterns that triggger self-sabotaging actions that can halt progress towwards our goals (see *Choosing You!* and *Time Rich Cash Optional: an unconventional guide to happiness* for more information on self-sabotage, visualisation and intentions.)

Action: Visualise your best-case life

Take a few minutes to sit comfortably in silence. Close your eyes and relax into a comfortable state (it may help to start with a few minutes of mindfulness-of-breath meditation). When you feel comfortable and centred ask yourself:

"How do I MOST want my life to be?"

As images, words, feelings and concepts arise, brainstorm them on a piece of paper (or journal). The things that you write down (or draw) are the frames that you use to explain (to yourself) and understand the life that you really want to be living.

The following triggers can be useful to get the process flowing:

Being

- Who do I want to be?
- What type of person do I want to be? (Happy, vivacious, empowered, strong, intelligent etc.)
- What type of life do I want to be living?
- What positive attributes do I already have? (Strength, wisdom, humour etc.)

Environment

- What does my perfect home or living situation look like?
- Where do I live?
- What is around me?

Relationships

- How do I want to be treated?
- How do I want to treat others?
- Who is with me? Who do I *want* to be with me?

Having

- What things do I have or possess?
- Why do I have these things in my perfect life?

Keep this piece of paper and if you want/need to, edit it and present the most important aspects of your perfect work-life scenario in a way that makes sense, and is emotionally compelling to *you*. I like lists and mind-maps (because I'm a 'word guy') but you may feel more comfortable with drawings or collages. Put your mind-map, collage or list somewhere that you will see it, like on a 'dream board' that is easily visible as you are planning and working to inspire you and keep you on track as you start into your awesome practice-life.

CREATING GREAT DAYS AT WORK

As we focus on what the most important concepts of our dream business are, it becomes imperative to evaluate what this would look like on a day-to-day basis. We can't begin to set the right goals (the ones that *actually* matter without first evaluating our core values and what the 'big picture' of our happiness looks like, nor can we begin to act day by day and moment by moment if we haven't evaluated what our perfect day in work, life and play is. In fact, the imagining and visualising of a perfect day is one of the exercises that I go back to most when I need a reminder of what it means for me to be really living—

as opposed to just getting by. Many of my clients have found this exercise to be one of the most important ones they have performed when creating their business and life schedule.

Action: What is your perfect day?

Take a moment to sit and relax. Become calm and centred and let yourself imagine a perfect day for *you*.

Start with how you would most like to rise in the morning:

How do you look?
How do you feel?
What is your mood, attitude and energy like?
What do you do first? Why?

Walk through the rest of your day, taking note of the key things that help you to create a perfect day of passion and purpose.

Remember this is your BEST CASE day—allow it to be awesome! Don't constrain your imagination.

After you have 'walked through' an entire day from rising to sleeping reflect on what you have imagined.

Am I currently living my perfect day?

What am I not doing that I could be doing right now?

What actions or activities could be easily implemented (no

additional time or money) right now?

(Hint—do these immediately!)

What other things could I, with a little planning, bring

into my day?

CHAPTER TWO

Time Rich Budgeting

Determining worth, value and time

"THE BUDGET IS NOT JUST A COLLECTION
OF NUMBERS, BUT AN EXPRESSION OF OUR
VALUES AND ASPIRATIONS."

~ JACOB LEW

Your needs, wants and desires determine how much you need to earn in order to live the life you've always dreamed of. This in turn determines the amount of *time* you are prepared (and able) to spend working and how much you need to charge for that time.

This chapter may seem slightly mercenary for a book about living a life of passion and purpose doing what you love, but a sound budget and sound financial goal-setting is critically important for conserving your energy and motivation levels for practice, for making sure that you have ample time to yourself, your family, friends, recreation and hobbies, and for having the resources to enjoy this time and to give back to others.

Without a budget you will be fighting an uphill

battle to truly enjoy your business…

OR your home life.

THE FAIR EXCHANGE PRINCIPLE

On several occasions I've written for magazines and blogs about the topic of how to monetise holistic, spiritual and other health services. I have often received reader feedback along the lines of: "Cliff, if you love what you do, and if you are working in the spiritual realm, then shouldn't it be freely available?"

Firstly, it is important to remember that I—like you—love what I do. In fact I wouldn't do it if I didn't, not even for all the money in the world. But I also choose to exist within the bounds of the society that we all co-create; one that relies on money as a medium for exhange. Whilst I believe that we can and should drastically change our societal perceptions around money, time and happiness, the fact remains that we all need money to purchase food, to pay rent, and to get from place to place. If I were to not charge for my services I wouldn't be able to service these very basic requirements, and would have to choose to either abandon society as we know it (which for some is a viable option) or take up another job—one which I would probably not get anywhere near as much life satisfaction from and which may not positively affect the lives of people in the same way that my current work does. In fact I would hazard a guess that if I were to retire from the field there would be at least a few people that would be disappointed. These are the people that are more than happy to pay for guidance, information, coaching and advice.

When we assume that because something is spiritual, health-promoting or holistic it should be free or cheap, we fall into a trap. In doing so we are separating the material/physical, mental/emotional and spiritual components of the human condition, when in fact they are intractably linked as interrelated components of all that we are.

Money is nothing but a medium of exchange. Viewed in this way the flow of money is analogous to a flow of energy.

In many years of mentoring others, I have seen many great practitioners drop out of the industry due to not feeling that they could charge at all, nor that they could charge what they are truly worth. In this loss we are all robbed of the amazing work that they could be doing.

A principle of the economy of spirituality and holism should be that of 'fair exchange'. When there is a fair exchange of energy, be that in the form of money, or payment in kind, there is a harmonious balance. In charging what we deserve we are valuing ourselves, just as in paying what is fair we are honouring and valuing the practitioner or other service provider, and allowing them to more comfortably express their passion to the world.

The fair exchange principle allows for free giving of goods and services and for many, many permutations of this. I, for example, give a proportion of all the revenue from my business to charity, and the proceeds of book sales and royalties to allow me more *time* to work with those that otherwise couldn't afford it. And like many other practitioners, offer a huge amount of freely available information in the form of blog posts, articles and 'pay by donation' plans and programs. It's all about a fair exchange.

Value is the key.

Valuing and honouring of the self and valuing and honouring those that may in turn guide us.

As you give, so shall you receive.

DETERMINING YOUR VALUE

What are you worth?

So far we have evaluated what it really means for us to have a business that we really love doing, one that fits within our values and ethos, and that provides for a life of ongoing passion and purpose. Now we need to start getting down to the 'nitty-gritty' of how this business actually works.

The absolute first thing we must do in this process is to determine what we are worth, and by extension what we are going to charge for our services.

When determining how much to charge and how much they should be earning, many practitioners would probably be better served gazing into a crystal ball than doing what they are currently doing (which is often little more than guessing...)

To determine what we need to be earning and charging, and how much we need to be working, we need to first know how much we are currently spending, and how much we will be spending over time.

Note: This is not your normal budgeting exercise!

Often budgeting has a self-limiting focus on 'pinching pennies' and looking at bare basic subsistence as a desired result, and it often puts expectations of what *should* be purchased. This mind-set of budgeting does NOT fit within our focus of Time Rich Practitioners. We are focused on eliminating unnecessary expenditure and creating the abundance that we require in order to be most effective in what we do, and identifying what is most important to spend our money on. In short; we are focused on health and on abundance of mind, body and spirit.

Your budget should be one that includes all of the things that you reasonably would like to have and do within a defined time-frame. I would suggest no shorter a time-frame than three months and no longer than 24 months. I only do budgeting and dream-setting exercises once per year. Too short a time-frame and you are unlikely to achieve any reasonable goals, too long a time-frame and there is too great a likelihood that unexpected life events, challenges and opportunities will cause you to have to re-evaluate anyway. Remember that over-preparing when other factors will inevitably force you to change that preparation anyway is a massive waste of your time!

Action: Create an effective budget and income calculator
For Dream-setting and budgeting I highly recommend using Tim Ferris's' Dream-setting calculator. You can download it for free here:
http://www.technotheory.com/download/DreamlineWorksheet2.0.xls
Note: You can also find Tim's book *The 4-Hour Workweek* at the Holistic Performance Nutrition recommended books page under 'Business Books':

http://www.holisticperformancenutrition.com/recommended-books.html

Fill in all the fields within the sheet, paying particular attention to all the experiences you would like to have in the coming year (or whichever time-frame you have indicated).

Once you have determined all of your costs, wants and needs you will have a good idea of what you will need to be earning per year, month and week.

The next step is to work out based on this what you need to be charging per hour.

BUT before you do this you'll need to decide how many hours you want to be working. Let me repeat: *Set how many hours you want to be working.* How much you will optimally work will be primarily dictated by energy and fatigue levels, not by how much anyone else works, or by how many hours the average (overworked and overstressed!) person works. For example, I really only want to work patient contact hours of around 10 per week. That may seem a little low, but I often give much more time to my clients than what has been allotted to their consultation time, and I give a lot of energy to my sessions and so if I consistently do more (let's say 20 or 30 hours) I end up becoming fatigued and over-stressed and when this happens I'm neither happy, nor am I giving the best to my clients.

It must be noted that I do a number of other things (like writing the book you are reading!) and so clinical practice isn't my only weekly priority. If it is for you, you may do a greater amount of hours or if you have other commitments, these will reduce your available and optimal working hours.

Action: Determine your hourly rate

1. Take your yearly income figure from the dream-line calculator

2. Divide by the amount of weeks you want to be working (I like to take around three months off per year so I work my hourly rate based on a 40 week year)

3. Then divide by how many days per week you want to be working and how many hours per day you can and want to put towards client contact hours

4. This gives you your hourly rate!

Example:

Bob needs to earn $88,000 dollars per year to satisfy his dream-line requirements. He also only wants to work a maximum of 20 client contact hours per week, and allow 6 weeks off per year for holidays. This equates to:

$$88,000 \div 46 \div 20 = (\text{rounded}) \ \$95 \text{ per hour}$$

Is this figure realistic?

Have you given yourself enough time off?

Are the hours worked per week too little or too much?

Evaluating the market in your particular field of industry and geographical area will give extra perspective on whether you are charging too little or too much, but always remember that there is a large variation in what people charge, and any client that comes to see you, is coming to see *you*. They are placing value in your service, and so should you.

CHAPTER THREE

Creating Brand 'You'

Building a brand that fits your practice

"THE MOST POWERFUL AND ENDURING BRANDS ARE BUILT FROM THE HEART. THEY ARE REAL AND SUSTAINABLE. THEIR FOUNDATIONS ARE STRONGER BECAUSE THEY ARE BUILT WITH THE STRENGTH OF THE HUMAN SPIRIT, NOT AN AD CAMPAIGN."

~ HOWARD SCHULTZ

Defining your brand is critical to understanding how you are going to position your business and therefore how you will begin to attract and engage a customer base. Your brand will, depending on how you create it, engage more or less effectively with different demographics.

Who you are, who you most want to work with, and how you want to be viewed in the world are some of the factors you may want to consider when you think about your brand identity.

IDENTIFYING YOUR STORY

Your personal story influences your brand identity and how you will ultimately appeal to and relate with your potential customers. It includes your challenges and triumphs, tragedies, and the unique and interesting experiences that set you apart from others.

It is not necessary to have climbed mountains, traversed deserts, won world championships or dated movie stars as part of your own story (although I can highly recommend all of the above!). The most important thing is to be 'real' and to identify and incorporate into your marketing material and copy the experiences from your own life journey that better enable you to help someone else. For example, having a solid and enduring relationship can certainly help if you are planning on relationship counselling being part of your practice, or having children if you are planning on working with kids.

I have Crohn's Disease and have been fortunate enough to work with and help many people with Inflammatory Bowel Diseases—because they can relate to my experiences. I have both the academic, personal and clinical qualifications and experience to be a) credible and b) effective.

What are your unique traits?

CREATING A GREAT BIO

Who are you?

What makes you unique?

Why would this encourage people to buy your product?

These are all questions that need to be asked in the process of setting up an effective business as a practitioner.

When creating a bio you are primarily searching for and finding the best way to explain your *Unique Selling Proposition* (USP). This is the thing that sets you apart, that makes you unique, and that people will relate to enough to want to give you their hard earned money in exchange for the service you provide.

Action: Create a great bio

You may just have one USP or perhaps a few, and there will undoubtedly be general and over-riding concept that defines what is most unique about you. Remember that the key point here is not just what is unique in the abstract, but what is unique *and will help you sell yourself to your target market*. In other words this is something that is unique to you, different to your potential competitors and appeals to your target audience.

What do you want to be as a brand?

This may seem unimportant, but in my business experience the 'feel' that we get from a brand is critical to how it will be perceived and even to how we will work within it. Taking a small amount of time to think about how you really want your brand to look and be perceived is a great way to solidify your brand identity and the core values and ethos of the business.

What are Your Credibility Indicators?

Credibility indicators are the qualifications, whether traditional or not, that will give your customers peace of mind that you know what you are doing. Of course this is not always the case and we all know of people who aren't 'qualified' in a traditional sense that do amazing work, and also those that have a veritable alphabet soup following their names who are simply diabolical. However, credibility indicators *are* something your clients will look to for some degree of security (pun intended!) and rightly so.

These 'credibility indicators' include:

- Traditional qualifications
- Degrees, diplomas and certificates
- Registrations

Registrations with professional certifying and registration bodies such as the Clinical Nutrition Association, Naturopathic Society, Register of Exercise Professionals (REPS) and others.

⚬ Non-traditional qualifications

Courses, seminars and workshops in complementary modalities

⚬ Continuing education

Courses, certificates and other education that provide Continuing Education Credits or Units (CECs/CEUs) for registering bodies such as the courses run by Holistic Performance Nutrition™.

(see www.holisticperformancenutrition.com)

⚬ Experience based credibility indicators

This includes your tenure (time in practice), case-types you've worked with, prominent people, interesting or challenging cases and personal experiences in work, life and athletics. For example:

Who have you worked with?

What have you done? (Athletic achievement, speaking, writing)

How long have you been in practice?

Having the outline of a bio isn't enough though. Your 'story' becomes a critical part of whether people are prepared to believe in, and 'buy in' to *you.*

Often my 'story' doesn't come up in every biographical reference point for my career and business, but it's a compelling aspect of who I am and why I do what I do. More importantly it is another critical touch-point that helps to make you more accessible to your target audience. In a nutshell, it makes you more human.

Action: Tell your story

If you were to write a (VERY SMALL!) novella about your life what would the key points be? Take a few moments to write down the most important and interesting aspects of your story and what makes you unique.

Remember to include your challenges and how you transcended them, your tragedies and what you learned from them, and your triumphs and unique anecdotes.

What are you?

Deciding what you most want to be doing in your practice allows you to be much more specific in your marketing, and be much clearer with your brand identity. Deciding 'what' you are as a practitioner involves more than just your vocational title— such as being a 'nutritionist'.

There are various modalities and specialist areas that any of us may choose to focus on within our practice. If you don't know what you want to focus on that is OK too, but if you have any sort of idea you should try to cast some attention on this and begin to 'hone down' on a theme, or just a few themes, of practice that allow you to be focussed in telling your story and getting your 'message' of practice out to your target market.

You can divide this up into several areas:

- Vocation

Primary (Example: 'Naturopath')

Secondary ('Clinical Nutritionist')

- Modalities

Primary (Nutritional Therapy)

Secondary (Mind-Body Therapy/Psych-K®)

What are your primary (and secondary if applicable) vocations and modalities?

What do you do?

Summarise exactly what you do in the shortest way possible! This is like a personal practice credo, otherwise known as a mission statement.

CHAPTER FOUR

Making Contact

Acquiring and engaging with new customers

"THERE IS ONLY ONE BOSS. THE CUSTOMER. AND HE CAN FIRE EVERYBODY IN THE COMPANY FROM THE CHAIRMAN ON DOWN, SIMPLY BY SPENDING HIS MONEY SOMEWHERE ELSE."

~ SAM WALTON

Acquiring customers is the key to beginning the cash flow in your business. Obviously without customers there is no revenue, and without customers there literally is no reason for you to be in business!

It must be noted though that acquisition is not ulitmately the key to maintaining cash flow, nor to the ultimate health of any business. As business author Dr Ian Brooks has counseled me on many occasions—the retention and maintenance of customers (as he calls it—their 'lifetime value') is more important, but suffice it to say that without making contact and engaging potential customers with a story that they can believe in, and a brand they can trust…you don't have anything to build upon.

YOU NEED A WEBSITE

Repeat: You must have a website!

Having an effective website is the first way that you can ensure that your clients can find you, and find out enough about you to entice them to book a session or seek further information. Even meeting people in-person and handing them your details physically in the form of a business card, flyer or pamphlet is now often not enough. Many consumers will either a) lose your business card and then 'google' you to find your details, or b) look for your website to check that you are the right 'fit' for them. Therefore if you don't have a website you have probably lost that customer.

Having a great looking website with all the 'bells and whistles' is great, but much more important is to have a website that works. I have, on countless occasions, worked with small business owners and practitioners who spend months or years attempting to put together the 'perfect' site, which often ends up not being very effective anyway. In the process of waiting for the perfect site they lose a lot of opportunities to expand their brand, educate customers and gain new clients. With website creation it is certainly true that perfection can be the enemy of progress!

> *You must have an effective online presence.*
>
> *Waiting for the perfect website will hurt you more than simply having a low-cost, good looking, effective website.*

Do it Yourself, or Have it Made?

I have, over the years, had many websites designed and built for me, and have also designed and built many myself. There are significant advantages and disadvantages to both outlined in the table below. Of course for anyone in a 'lean start-up' business in which there is little available cash for building online or physical infrastructure, the only option is a self-built design in one of the many high-quality, third-party online applications. I have enjoyed building sites in Weebly, Wix, Typepad, Blogger and other platforms, and have found the sites that I've created to be every bit as good as expensive custom sites. Sometimes they can suit the start-up business owner better because they are easier for me to change and customise as needed as the young business grows and changes.

	Self-built	Custom design and build
Ease of design and build	Easy	N/A
Cost	Low-cost	Significant build costs, may be significant ongoing design costs (depending on the ease of use of the CMS)
Time cost (to you)	High – time must be allocated to the project. Is this worth the opportunity cost?	N/A
Time to completion (lag time)	Often low – template and 'build it yourself' builders usually offer an easy way to have an online presence quickly	Design and build times are often considerable. It all depends on the web designer, but in my experience many of the people I have mentored have had significant delays and a long build time to get their site online.

Which Site Builder Should You Use?

Weebly – www.weebly.com

A great option if you want a variety of add-ons and the ability to easily incorporate shopping, online booking and custom membership functions. It has a clean and simple interface with many templates. Weebly also has great form functionality so you can have online intake forms and pre-screens that are filled in online and emailed directly to you.

Holistic Performance Nutrition is built using the Weebly platform: www.holisticperformancenutrition.com

Wix – www.wix.com

Wix used to be a flash site builder. This was great if you wanted to a very 'rich' looking site, and I must say some of the sites built with Wix are quite beautiful. Unfortunately Flash sites struggle with SEO optimisation (although it is getting much better) and some sites have trouble with deep linking and they can't be viewed (easily) on iPads and iPhones. Wix now has an HTML5 site option so you can build a great looking, feature rich site in HTML. Not quite as functional as Weebly in my opinion but a great option for a very slick looking website.

Other options to consider:

Squarespace – www.squarespace.com

Great looking, functional sites for a low cost.

Training Tilt – www.trainingtilt.com

An interesting option offering a site-builder with client engagement tools and online programming. Designed initially as a tool for coaches and trainers (with an endurance focus), it is now gaining more functionality for nutritionists ansd other practitioners.

Action: Create a simple website

Go to one of the site-builders above and set up a free account. PLAY. Just get stuck-in and play around with creating some pages. Don't go so far down the process that you actually build your site, but become familiar with the functionaltiy and the operation of customising pages. Most importantly make sure that the builder you are using can do what you require and that you find it simple and intuitive to use. If you don't like that builder try another one until you come up with your unique best fit.

Tips:

    ⚬   **Use GREAT images for your site**.
One of the things that most impacts how a site looks is the quality of the images. Also be aware of copyright when using images. For site images I tend to err on the side of caution and buy them from a stock photo store such as iStock Photo – www.istockphoto.com

    ⚬   **Plan your site**
A simple sketch or flow chart on a piece of paper is enough to begin with, or a Microsoft PowerPoint slide graphically representing your site is a great way to plan it out too. Note: this is also a great visual representation of how you want your site to look that

you can take to a designer for full customisation or for
occasional coding work if need be.

◎ Take inspiration from others

Look around at other sites that are similar to what you
would like. Feel free to borrow ideas and concepts liberally!

A great looking, highly functional website need not be
expensive, and can easily be created by anyone using these
tools. Don't get stuck in limbo without a website!

CHAPTER FIVE

Making an Impact

Content marketing and visibility

"MARKETING IS A CONTEST FOR PEOPLE'S ATTENTION."

~ SETH GODIN

You can make contact, and you can gain new customers, but neither of these is enough if you can't retain customers, continue to acquire customers over the long term, and engage these customers individually and as a community.

To do this requires making an impact, and there is no better way to create an impact in your field by putting out great content. Content that educates, informs and entertains sets you apart from your peers. It's a gift that you can give to your clients, but it's a gift that continues to feed back to you time and time again.

Everyone tells you that you must have a blog…I mean I just finished telling you that you MUST have a website (which is true)…BUT you don't *need* a blog! A blog *can* be very helpful to help to educate your clients and visitors to your site, to engage them and to position yourself as a more credible expert. Of course the material that you are putting up needs to be of a high quality, and you need to be inspired and excited to write it. If you're not, stop now, skip this section and move on! Writing articles is not for everyone, and it may be a better use of your time to engage and educate in different ways. Bear in mind that you can always repost articles and material by people that you respect and follow in the field too, or over time you might be able to use other content (such as filmed presentations or podcasts) and either post these as multi-media posts or have them transcribed by a virtual assistant (more about these later) to gain more content.

If you do want to blog or write articles there are several platforms on which to do this:

Blogging on Your Own Site

The site builders mentioned above have easy-to-use and effective blogs. They work well, are seamlessly integrated with your site, and will improve the SEO ranking of your site by incorporating text rich content within it.

Using Hosted (3rd Party) Blogs

The blogs contained within web builders like those above aren't always as feature rich, nor have as many add-ons as some of the specific blog engines like WordPress (www.wordpress.org and www.wordpress.com – for self-hosted and hosted blogs/sites respectively), Blogger (www.blogger.com) or TypePad (www.typepad.com). These blog sites can also be used as vary effective sites in and of themselves, and in the case of WordPress sites (the generic non-hosted version) have become somewhat of an industry standard for site creation.

Blogging for Other Sites

Posting content to other blogs and communities serves several purposes:

1) It increases your visibility online

2) Visibility is (rightly or wrongly) equated with credibility and

3) It drives traffic to your site through direct linking and people searching for you after reading the post or article.

This is a great option for anyone that wishes to write, whether they want to have their own blog or not. Something to remember is that once you have written content it can be reposted, reused and changed in the future to fit a different format. It could form the basis of a future article or even an idea or content for a book project.

If you want to go down this route take a look at some of the most visited and most credible blog and content sites in your field and think of article ideas that you could write that fit within their scope and tone. Try to pick out high impact websites and make sure that if you write an article that you link to it from your site and social media platforms, and that they also link back to you. This 'back-linking' is a great way to improve your search engine optimisation (SEO) rankings for engines such as Google.

Be aware that over time as your visibility increases (and especially if you have a 'knack' for writing) people will approach you to write content for them. IF you need business and you could benefit from the exposure then feel free to do this as a contra (or gratis) in lieu of an advertising or marketing cost, but if you are already busy, it is crazy to take up your hard earned time writing for free! I often have magazines, websites and blogs approaching me to write for them and many of them often say something to the effect of "We can't pay you anything, but it'll be great for your business!" The reality is that I am too busy anyway! And so to serve my clients, students and paying customers effectively I can't afford to take on writing work unless it's paid and paid well.

Don't work for free unless you can see a real and tangible benefit in doing so.

Action: Write an article for a 3ʳᵈ party blog or website

1. Do a search using online tools for some of the most visited sites in your field.

2. Visit as many of these as possible and determine which ones fit within your scope of practice and fit with your ethos and values.

3. Brainstorm some ideas of articles you would love to write for one or more of these sites.

4. Decide on your three top ideas

5. Outline an article idea for each of these. Write a punchy title and intro for the article and a synopsis of the articles message and intention.

6. [Now things get a little scary!] Contact the editor or submissions contact for the website with your idea.

7. Fingers crossed your idea will be accepted. If not, make sure that you reply to the editor thanking them for their time and let them know that you have additional ideas for articles and ask if they have anything that they would like written. Remember that you can always approach other sites with your article ideas if not accepted by your first choice and you can use your articles at your own site too whether accepted or not.

Tools:

www.alexa.com

Alexa provides data on the most visited websites worldwide, by category and by country.

Social Media and Your Online Presences

Social media and other 3rd party platforms give you another level of visibility, a chance to tell your story, and most importantly a chance to engage and interact with you clients and potential clients.

Some of these platforms include:

About.me – www.about.me

A nice splash-page for saying a little about you and directing people to your other social media and websites. Note: This can be also be an excellent proxy website if you are in the process of building something more substantial or only need a basic online presence.

Example: www.about.me/cliffharvey

Facebook – www.facebook.com

The king of social media, with over 1.23 billion monthly active users[1], Facebook is the most widely and ubiquitously used social media platform on the planet.

Twitter – www.twitter.com

Twitter was the first uber-successful 'micro-blogging' platform.

Instagram – www.instagram.com

Instagram is a social sharing site for images. Demographically it has a younger audience than both Twitter and Facebook and has higher numbers of visits per day. Due to its integration with the heavily used Instagram photo app it is primarily used for sharing self-taken images.

Pinterest – www.pinterest.com

Pinterest has over 4 times as many women users as men. It is—like Instagram—an image sharing portal and so is particularly popular for sharing images, quotes-as-images, and recipes (a particularly popular and powerful way to spread content for nutritionists and naturopaths!).

YouTube – www.youtube.com

The preeminent video portal on the web. This google owned company has become the place to post and view videos online

---

[1] http://investor.fb.com/releasedetail.cfm?ReleaseID=821954

and has a major effect on search engine rankings and general online visibility. It also integrates seemlessly with Google+ and its suite of apps (such as Google Hangouts, which is a great way to engage with your clients and potential customers via webinars and podcasts).

Common Mistakes

Mistake #1: Trying to engage via every social media channel

Don't make the common mistake of thinking that you have to be active and involved in ALL social media. To do so, unless it's all that you want to do, is just too time consuming.

In practice most people I have worked with find that they can only really be effective consistently using three social or content media platforms or less. I have dubbed this the 'Rule of Three' and have found it to be a great razor for action. If you try to do all things, all the time you won't do anything well.

For example I use Facebook heavily, Twitter moderately and variously use *either* Instagram or Pinterest only occasionally.

Mistake #2: Using platforms you don't enjoy

A question inevitably arises: Which social medium is *best* for me to use?

When asked this question I go against the grain. Often you'll be given statistics and figures about which SM platform has the most users, the highest engagement or the most 'traction' within your target demographic.

But I'm specifically going to tell you to NOT simply look into which one has the greatest numbers, the greatest supposed ROI (return on investment) or the which is growing most rapidly or is the next 'big thing'.

Social media is fun…or at least it should be! And so you should use what is most FUN to you. If you love Facebook then spend a little time building your Facebook brand page and engaging with people on it. If you love Twitter then tweet really cool stuff and then talk to people about it. If you love beautiful images then Pinterest could be the best option to focus on, and if you love taking photos then Instagram is a no-brainer.

Bottom line – let your passion show through!

Focusing on fun and passion will help you to engage more authentically and avoid the trap of thinking that a social media marketing strategy is a cynical ploy focused only on sales and dollars.

Mistake #3: Selling without engaging

If there's one thing I really HATE it's when businesses talk about how they can *use* social media to get more sales. I understand, I get it…cash flow is our key priority in business. BUT in a Time Rich business it's certainly not the only priority, and that's why you're reading this—time , enjoyment and giving back to our communities are all equally important too!

I find it very cynical to simply be trying to sell via our engagements and to have that as our implicit bias for doing it, to the point where it can actually be quite manipulative. I believe though that by using social media that you enjoy, and by creating and being involved with conversations that you love to be a part of, you will have a much better result than simply trying to sell something. You will more than likely engage with people on a deeper and more personal level too, and this can only enhance the foundations of your business and practice over time.

Mistake #4: Posting poor content

There seems to be so much attention paid to optimal posting times and frequency of posting that at least some people feel obliged to post content, even if that content isn't great quality.

My advice: forget about frequency of posting or optimal times and simply focus initially on consistently creating great articles, images, infographics or other media that people will actually get some benefit from!

Great content is the way to become a credible expert AND to positively change people's lives, each and every day. This drives a desire from your market for more information and rest assured people will seek you out for personal help and/or will buy your products.

Remember that when you are 'giving away' content you are in fact trading your content for someone's valuable time. They take a risk when deciding to click on your link and read your article. They are sacrificing time they could be doing something else with. Honour their time by puting out *great* work.

Tip: A great way to find interesting content for your audience is to set up some simple google or google scholar alerts. These send an email daily (or at your specified time interval) with relevant posts and articles direct to your inbox.

Mistake #5: Broadcasting, not conversing

Take a look at some corporate Facebook pages. You will see post after post by the company and not one reply to comments in the ensuing threads. It leaves you feeling as if someone is merely talking at you, instead of with you. And that's exactly what is happening.

When we post any content we are trying to a) educate, b) engage and further educate, and c) learn more about our craft and our business through the process of online, social engagement. I have learnt as much from my clients and patients over the years as they have from me. We seek to not simply to to our community, but to deepen relationships with, and within it.

Bottom line: When you post on social media, be prepared to start a conversation with your community.

Answer questions, respond to critiques and generally just be cool…like the Fonz!

Posting GREAT content is the number one way to have people engage with you, but then having conversations with them, answering questions and being a real-live human being are what helps people to relate to you, and also to trust you enough to buy your services or products.

Mistake #6: Not giving

Give that little bit more. Not just the content you are posting, but answers to queries, perhaps some free information, downloads or other content. Giving makes you feel good (and that should be reason enough to do it) but there are also financial benefits. When we give we create gratitude within the person and they are more likely to then pay in future for our services. We also create a situation of instantaneous trust and this encourages more long-term engagement and the potential to create a 'lifelong customer'.

Action: Creating and finding great content

- Brain storm some of the terms that could apply to you and your practice. For example, I am involved in ongoing research into ketogenic and lower-carbohydrate, higher-fat diets and so I have set search terms in google scholar for terms such as 'ketosis' and 'low-carb'

- To set up a google scholar alert simply open up google scholar (www.scholar.google.com) search for your term and then click on the 'create alert' button on the left.

- To set up a standard google alert go to www.google.com/alerts and enter your search terms (make sure that you are logged in to your google account.)

Tools:

For more information on using FREE check out *Free: The Future of a Radical Price Point* by Chris Anderson.

Free copies available here:

https://archive.org/details/FreeTheFutureOfARadicalPrice

To find out more about social and market norms check out *Predictably Irrational* by Dan Ariely at the recommended books section of HPN:

http://www.holisticperformancenutrition.com/recommended-books.html

Great information on the value of a long-term customer can be found in Dr Ian Brooks' books here: http://www.ianbrooks.com

Use social media management tools to save time and increase reach

Even if you are sticking with the 'Rule of Three' (which I highly recommend) it can still be time consuming to consistently post to social media and to monitor and engage effectively. Social media management tools like Hoot Suite (my favourite) help to make this process a lot easier. In a nutshell social media platforms like Hoot Suite allow you to aggregate all your social media 'feeds' into one platform so that you can see, at-a-glance everything that is going on in real time. It also offers aggregated push notices that can be sent to your various devices and has a great App for both iOS and Android.

An additional reason to use management tools is the ability to set up streams within your dashboard that monitor the various social media platforms (such as Facebook and Twitter) for search terms. So, for example, I have streams set up within Hoot Suite that show me when things like #lowcarb and #ketosis are mentioned and my team are also notified whenever our company and products are mentioned.

Tools:

Hoot Suite – www.hootsuite.com

Online Directories

Signing up to several of the many health and wellness directory sites is an easy way to have a greater online presence. My advice though is to NEVER pay for the premium listings (it's just money down the drain) but the free listings are an easy, no-cost, low time-input way to increase the amount that your brand will be seen, and the linking to your website will help to drive up search engine rankings.

Magazines

A LOT of my exposure in the media has come from magazines. In the early years of my practice I met some people involved in producing various sports and fitness magazines and in spite of having no professional writing experience, I took a leap into the unknown and started writing. If I look back on some of my earliest articles I am embarrassed…(they are god-awful!) but they helped me to hone the craft of writing, which has become an integral part of my current business (books, copy-writing, article writing) and an area that pays very well. Not only that but the exposure and 'credibility indicator' I gained from being featured in magazines in New Zealand, Australia, Canada and the United States helped to solidify my standing as a 'key opinion leader' in the health and performance area.

Television and Radio

Television appearances aren't the Holy Grail. I've been featured on television a bunch of times as a health expert and as an athlete (I used to lift heavy things…) and the Kardashians still aren't beating down my door to date me. It has been a nice boost to my presence and visibility though. Like writing, most of the hard work is actually in saying 'YES!' to opportunities and overcoming the fear of being in front of the microphone or camera. And hey—even if it's a total disaster they can never take away that you have been a featured expert on radio and TV!

Guest Lectures and Workshops

Guest lectures are a great credibility indicator, especially if done for academic organisations and major corporate players. Again the challenge is often in taking the plunge and doing it. Crafting a presentation is a skill in itself, and having the confidence and security to speak to larger groups can be a hard challenge to summount. But the results can be well worth it if this is an area you'd like to develop in your practice-business.

Action: Organise a workshop, promote it, and do it!

1. Think of a topic that would help to answer a key question that your target market have. Use the 'Start With Why' method to determin a powerful topic that is relevent to your audience.

2. Plan out a simple 40 minute presentation.

3. Decide what to charge.

4. Organise the event, finding a venue, time, and a date.

5. Use an online booking engine (such as EventBrite – www.eventbrite.com) to take bookings

6. Promote your workshop via Facebook, emails and other social media.

CHAPTER SIX

Becoming Effective

Do what serves best, and discard the rest

"EFFICIENCY IS DOING THINGS RIGHT; EFFECTIVENESS IS DOING THE RIGHT THINGS."

~ PETER DRUCKER

Being time efficient doesn't really mean anything…

I know that everyone seems to talk about it—but if you're being really efficient at doing all the wrong things, or even worse a whole bunch of things that don't even matter, you're simply wasting more time. A better concept is to become super-effective. Effectiveness lies in doing the most important things, discarding the unimportant and then having the straetgies to make the important things easier to do, in a shorter time. Many concepts we have already evaluated, but in this chapter we will extend this even further.

A key to becoming more time effective (in other words having more time for you) is to have a structure that you can use to eliminate tasks from your to-do list and from your inbound communications (like email.)

There are some simple tricks you can use to become a time magician.

THE '4 DS' OF TIME EFFECTIVENESS

Any task that comes to you can be dealt with using the four 'Ds' of time effectiveness—adapted loosely from *Getting Things Done* by David Allen and expanded upon in my second book *Time Rich Cash Optional: an unconventional guide to happiness*. Both books can be found at the Holistic Performance Nutrition bookstore: www.holisticperformancenutrition.com/recommended-books.html

1. DUMP

2. DO

3. DELEGATE

4. DEFER

Dump

The first thing you should ask yourself when looking at an item on your to-do list or in your inbox is "Does this need to be done?" Be VERY cut-throat with this. ANYTHING that doesn't absolutely need to be done for compliance (accounts and taxes), revenue creation (your business) or enjoyment you should simply throw out immediately.

The sense of freedom from simply deleting something is quite amazing. Deleting emails is one of my favourite things to do!

Do

Do the important and the easy (low time-cost) things right now.

Uncompleted tasks are a mental burden that sits in the back of our minds creating latent stress and worry. The crazy thing is that many of the things that we put off, and much of what is sitting in our inbox and on our to-do lists, are things that could be done in under 2 minutes!

The time to do these things (assuming they need to be done—according to point #1 'Dump') is so much less than the extra time to defer them and the mental stress of having them left uncompleted. A simple rule is that if a task comes across your desk (or cyber desk) that will take less than five minutes to complete, do it, and do it now.

Delegate

Question: Why would you do something if someone else could do it more effectively or at less financial or time cost?

Learning to delegate tasks is one of the keys to success for freeing up your time. And in the modern age of new media and new commerce, many options to delegate are at little or no cost.

Knowing what to delegate, to whom, and to focus your efforts saves you time, but more-importantly, allows you to fill your valuable time with the things that are most enjoyable and rewarding (in the long run it can really save you money as well)…which really is the ultimate win-win...win!

Action: Determine what needs to be done…and what doesn't

1. Make a list of all your daily and weekly tasks
2. Determine what you absolutely must do manually
3. For all other tasks define what can be delegated to software and what needs to be delegated to a person.

Note: ALWAYS delegate to automated software solutions where able before delegating to outsourced or internal staff. They are almost always cheaper, more 'scalable' (they grow with your business) and are more future proof (i.e. they won't leave you!)

Some of the strategies already mentioned are examples of delegating to software. There are many more.

For tasks and actions that need to be performed by someone there are several options available to you:

1. Hire people 'in-person'

2.   Outsource to virtual assistants

3.   Take on interns

I use all three strategies. I have a great personal assistant and office manager (Katherine you rock!) as well as two graphic and web designers in the Philippines who do excellent work at low cost to me—but high reward to them. For example, I pay my designers between 8 and 12 US dollars an hour compared to the average income of around $2.50 (rounded up and based on statistics from the Philippines Government Statistics Authority[2]).

In the first instance though you will have a) less need for help and b) will be running your practice on the smell of an oily rag. Do whatever you need to do yourself when cash flow is tight…but as soon as you can afford to, hire an outsourcer to take away those tasks that are non-rewarding to you and your passion/purpose or that take away your valuable time.

You can hire low-cost, high quality designers, virtual assistants (VAs), data miners (for compiling info and databases) and more on a 'one off' basis on sites like e-lance or ODesk or you can hire VAs on an ongoing basis.

---

[2] http://www.nscb.gov.ph/secstat/d_income.asp

Action: Try outsourcing

Identify a job that needs to be completed within your business that you don't have the time or skillset to do and that you can't afford to pay someone locally to do.

1. Work out a budget that you are happy to pay for this job or project.
2. Go to Odesk or E-Lance and post your job.
3. Make sure your brief is concise, written in plain, practical English and describes exactly (but succinctly!) what you need done.
4. Evaluate potential applicants and hire someone.

Set strict parameters around how long the task should take, and set weekly time limits if needed. Don't make this first job a long or complicated one. The key of this exercise is to get used to outsourcing, don't let it get away from you and cost too much money!

Tools:

Elance – www.elance.com

ODesk – www.odesk.com

99 Designs – www.99designs.com (a great site for posting one-off design projects with a budget.)

Websites like Elance (www.elance.com) and others make it easy to have freelance professionals bid for projects for which you previously may have had little option but to pay top dollar for. Online solutions in accounting, logistics, publishing and marketing are providing low- and, in many cases, no-cost options.

Outside of increased cash flow and time, an often underestimated benefit of delegating is that you simply don't have to do things you don't want to do.

For example, if you can't stand doing accounts then I would suggest you don't do them. Any task that provides mental stress and anguish that you can realistically afford to have done by someone else you should delegate. If you can't afford to, you have two options: 1. find a way to be able to afford it, or 2. find a viable, lower cost solution.

In the modern economy there may be ways you can simplify other areas of your life or business so you are able to delegate the tasks you don't enjoy. This can often provide additional stress-reducing benefits of simplification.

Defer

Having tasks sitting around without any sort of end date, conclusion or plan plays on your mind, and while it may not always be taking your time directly, it certainly can provide residual stress and anxiety that can affect the quality and enjoyment of your time. But as soon as there is some type of resolution to the problem (even if the task is not finished) much of the anxiety is put to rest. Simply having set aside a time to do the task takes away the thoughts of 'when am I going to do this?'

By writing it down and making it time-accountable we remove it from our mental to-do list. This has a profound effect and is why writing things down, having a schedule, and making lists of things to do is so important—it removes the obligation to remember everything.

Deferring tasks does not mean just putting them to one side. When we defer a task, if we simply put it on the back burner, it still hangs around as mental rubbish tapping our energy. When we defer a task or activity we must make it time-accountable. This brings us back to time-blocking. When we are unable to either dump, delegate or do a task, we must find a time when we could do it, then diarise that time for the task. That way it is dealt with and no longer remains something we have to worry about—until it becomes a 'do' task. Until that time, at least, mentally we can let it go.

For more information on Time Effectiveness I highly recommend: *Getting Things Done: The Art of Stress-Free Productivity* by David Allen.

CHAPTER SEVEN

Creating More Time

Becoming an effectiveness magician

"THEY ALWAYS SAY TIME CHANGES THINGS, BUT YOU ACTUALLY HAVE TO CHANGE THEM YOURSELF.."

~ ANDY WARHOLE

We may not work any harder or longer than we did 50 years ago, but we certainly work very differently. This difference in work—with more work distractions, more instantaneous communication tools and less defined work roles are considered to have driven a large increase in latent stress levels. For this reason gaining some sanity and clarity around your daily planning is an important, and very necessary way to ensure that you are being effective and reaching your goals, and also protecting your valuable time for other pursuits and preserving your energy.

Create To-Do List Sanity

One of the most important things you can do to free up your time and mental energy is to have a daily to-do list and one or more general or project specific to-do lists.

The reason for this is that if you only have one to do list you will always feel like you're never getting anything done! Having smaller to-do lists that are day and task specific gives a feeling of completion, and a sense of closure at the end of any given day that drastically reduces stress.

The optimal strategy is to have a general to-do list that you dump everything into (and/or a number of project specific to-do lists) and then a daily to-do list. I call my daily to-do list my 'Mission Critical' list. This mission critical list is the stuff that you absolutely must get done in that day.

The problem with a normal to-do list is the you either just work your way down from the top (ineffective) randomly decide what to do (even more ineffective!) or pick just the stuff you 'want' to do that day or is easy to do (ineffective!!!).

A mission critical list allows you to pick at least one important task or action to do in your day and one to two urgent tasks. Important tasks are the ones that lead towards larger life and business goals. This could be writing a book, preparing content for presentations or workshops or business planning for the future (note: it is *never* replying to emails). Urgent tasks are several of the myraid tasks that need to be done within a short time frame. Sometimes these are projects within your larger life goals, or sometimes they are simply compliance tasks (like doing taxes). I will talk more about 'imortant vs. urgent' in the next section.

Once the tasks in your mission critical list are done you have accomplished all that you 'need' to do in that day. The feeling of freedom and accomplishment this provides is amazing. You finish the tasks and immediately you're a winner! And the nicest thing is that you can then either stop for the day, do creative, fun business stuff (play!) or work on other things in your general or specific to-do lists so that you feel like you're ahead of the game. Compare this to how you usually feel when looking at your to-do list, even if you do manage to get a lot done in a day….you feel as if there's still so much more to do, which can be extremely demoralising.

Action: Organise your to-do list
1) Split your to-do list into 'general' and 'mission-critical'
2) Put everything into your general list
3) Pick **no more than three** tasks that you will do tomorrow and put them into your mission-critical list
   Note: These three tasks are the things you absolutely (no ifs, buts or maybes) *will* do tomorrow.

Tools:
There are several great apps that can help to better organise your to-do lists. The best of these also allow your lists to be available across all your devices.

Note: don't let all the various the organisational features of any app distract you. Keep your to-do lists and your personal organisation strategy as simple as it can possibly be in order for you to get the job done—no more.

My favourite to-do apps are:

- Google Keep
- Any.do
- Trello

All these apps are available in the Apple iStore, Google Play and for Windows and Mac.

'Block' Your Time

Creating 'time-blocks' for activities in your daily schedule is one of the easiest ways to become more effective with your time. Time-blocking is simply setting aside a certain period of time and deciding to do only one task within that time. Sounds simple, right?

Well, it is simple, but all too often we get distracted by the myriad tasks we have to complete, and we switch from one thing to another – dissipating our effectiveness and reducing our focus and productivity.

Procrastination and aversion also affect our ability to truly focus and 'get down to business'. When we don't want to do something (even if it's something we know we really *should* do) there are many ways we delay actually doing it.

Pushing 'send and receive' on your email program, checking Instagram, Facebook and Twitter accounts and perusing the headlines on Google news are just a few of the ways to delay the inevitable.

All of these things, whilst probably a little enjoyable, are not necessarily helping us *in the moment* to get the most out of our time.

Blocking out time is extremely simple. If you have to get a project done, simply set an amount of time aside and within that time focus solely on one task. Set your watch, or set a timer, and work away on the project without distraction, until the end of the time-block, then if you choose you can have a break or switch to something else…or check those pesky emails…

For writing projects you could set a word limit rather than a time-block, or you could simply decide that a 'must do' task or achievement has to be completed before you can do anything else with your day. Or you could use any other *defined* and *quantifiable* measure for your 'block'. Once you've decided on what you're going to do the only thing you need to do is sit down and actually do it!

I have found the most effective way for me to set aside time for writing is to simply prioritise it in my daily schedule and set a word count (usually 500-1000 words) that I must achieve before I can turn my mind to other tasks. Even if the words I am putting on paper are not my best work (they can after all be editted later), they provide the framework, and the 'critical mass' of information for my articles, books and lectures. My great friend and mentor Dr Ian Brooks gave me, when writing my first book, sage advice that I have carried with me since that day. He told me: "Finish your draft". He said many aspiring authors get hung up on writing, editing and rewriting *parts* of their book, without ever finishing a draft. In other words, they were honing the details without ever reaching the critical mass of information required to have a 'book'. This is true of any project and that's why giving it the time to simply make sure there is a solid base of work, information and material is crucial to success.

There are, of course, times when I can be extremely motivated, inspired and creative, and it is at these times I write more and of a better quality too; however, if I only wrote during those times of energy and motivation, I would get no writing projects finished at all.

'Boundless energy is not a requirement for achieving your goals, but boundless perseverance is!'
~ *From* Choosing You!

Do the Single Most Important Thing in Your Day First!
Whenever I have been at my most productive, and more importantly at my most *effective*, I have applied this rule in some form.

We often get 'bogged down' by the inevitably long list of things that become attracted to our to-do lists, and the cycle of slowly working our way through them can be confusing and at times even a little soul-destroying! In reality, though, much of what is on our to-do list is not so much important, as necessary. In other words, many of the tasks we have to do are simply related to compliance or have been left so long as to become urgent; however, they are not necessarily the things a) we either have a passion for doing, or b) that will help put us where we want to be in life.

For many of these tasks I would highly recommend a cut-throat application of the four Ds outlined earlier (especially the dumping and delegating portions), and for the rest I suggest choosing just one (or at most four, with less than three being preferable) task that is critical in any given day. It should be the thing that if you did only that—and nothing else—you would feel happy with your day.

Many people have written about similar themes, and I have found from experience, because I like to have a single focus (as it keeps my somewhat scattered and ethereal nature in check … and because it allows me the potential to get to the beach a little earlier!), that simply having one mission-critical task in any given day works extraordinarily well. It might be, for me, that I write a certain number of words on my current book, blog post or magazine article, or that I spend a certain amount of time on a research project. Of course it is very seldom the only thing I do in a given day, but it *is* what I deem to be the most important, and by setting it up as such, I must make sure it is completed and given its due importance in my mind's eye and in my schedule.

The laser-like focus that the *one thing today* rule allows, is to reduce the potential for us to get stuck doing low return, and often draining activities, such as checking email (possibly the worst thing you can do first thing in the day) or Facebook, or finding ourselves in the awful position of having wasted a day doing non-time-critical chores at the expense of doing the things we are passionate about.

Often doing the important things presents a block for us because if we actually start to work on projects we hold dear to our very core being, we become committed to them. This is a very challenging position, because when we begin to work towards our dreams we open ourselves up to criticism. We fear that if we create something it will not be seen as good enough by others, and we fear we won't be able to make money from our efforts in creative or expression-based fields. We fear the loss of feelings of security if we begin to stray from the norm. All these fears are valid, but if we do not put time and effort into the things that matter to us, we instead put time and effort into things that are inconsequential. This is a complete waste of our most precious resource. It matters not what the artist does, except for doing her art. It matters not what others think of the 'art' or the 'work' because she can only do that for which she craves.

If It's Important Do It Every Day

Doing the important thing/s first in your day is a great way to ensure that they actually get done, but just doing something once or twice is seldom enough to complete any of the larger tasks you may have set, or to gain knowledge or learn a skill well. Consistency is the key to learning new skills and to achieving the larger goals we may set. I am by nature a 'sprinter'. I like to work extremely hard for sustained periods of time and then rest. But no matter how fast we 'sprint' we can't always achieve all worthwhile goals in one burst of intense activity, and so we need to be consistent in working towards the goal…and the best way to do this is to do a little bit each and every day.

When eating an elephant take one bite at a time…
~ Creighton Abrams

Action: Do one thing every day for the next 21 days

1. Consider the following seven areas of life: Physical health, mental and emotional health, spirituality and personal growth, relationships (family, friends and your social life), finances and career, fun and recreation, and creativity.

2. Rate each area in your life between 1 (pretty crap really…) and 10 (awesome!)

3. What is the lowest rated area in your life?

4. What is a daily action that you could perform each and every day, first thing upon rising that would help to improve this area?

5. Set a plan to start first thing tomorrow. If you need to set up your environment or get any equipment to enable your goal *do it now*. (Seriously—I mean it, go and get it now!)

6. Each and every morning for the next 21 days perform that action.

'Batch' Time for Communication

It is crucial to set time aside for the important things that we most want to be doing with our days and to prioritise these. But of course it is also crucial to actually get done some of the compliance-based activities in our days. The way we can deal with this is outlined in the four Ds of time effectiveness; however, one thing that distracts us is communication. This used to involve mainly email communication but now also includes all the various social media.

I *love* social media. I think social networking is super-cool, and it gives me a great way to stay connected to my clients, friends and readers all over the world at the touch of a button. But it can also be used as a tool for distraction and procrastination. What is an amazing conduit for connection can easily become a replacement for real human interaction and a distraction from what is really most important for us to be doing.

Setting aside time for communications is a great way to deal with this.

Set aside a defined time (I typically do all my communications at 11 am and 4 pm, for example) to clear emails, check Facebook and Twitter, and post to social media or your blog, and make sure you *do* actually 'clear' emails and other online communication, not just peruse it.

When doing this I am more focused on replying to people (a good thing), connecting, and I still allow myself time to 'play' online as well. It's the best of both worlds.

Don't 'Work' if There is Nothing to do!

This concept also seems simple – right?

I can almost hear you saying, "Why would I work when there's nothing to do? I don't do that …"

But don't be so sure. Have there ever been times when you have sat at your computer, staring at the screen, trying to get some energy or inspiration from somewhere, or clicking 'send and receive' or 'refresh' on your email programme, waiting for the crucial last piece of information needed for you to complete a project?

During these episodes you're not really working, and you're certainly not having fun, so you are wasting time. If you're not able to be productive you are better off doing something else or simply taking time to relax and chill out.

Don't Work if You're Not Being Productive

Sometimes you have a to-do list as long as your arm and you know that you should be working. But you are tired, unmotivated or you just can't get a clear idea of a way forward with a particular task. At these times it can be better to stop and do something else, or simply rest until you can move forward more effectively.

Commitment to a task, work ethic and getting 'stuck in' are all imperative for accomplishing things, but we also need to be pragmatic. If you are not making headway on a task you might be better off taking a break.

If I find myself with writer's block, or not being productive for more than a few minutes, I stop and take a break. Often if I'm tired from training or not getting enough sleep, I'll do one of my favourite things: siesta, or I'll go for a walk, meditate, go to the gym or even better, take myself out on a solo date where I do something I have wanted to do—like go to the local art gallery or to a movie. Even a small break when you are feeling like everything is getting on top of you can be enough to kick-start your creative fire and give you the energy you need to launch yourself back into your day with gusto.

CHAPTER EIGHT

Automate

Making it work without you

"NEVER AUTOMATE SOMETHING THAT CAN BE ELIMINATED, AND NEVER DELEGATE SOMETHING THAT CAN BE AUTOMATED OR STREAMLINED."

~ TIMOTHY FERRISS

Once you have acquired customers and you have a steady stream of people coming in the door to purchase your products and services your next priority should be to maximise your available time and effectiveness.

Wasting time is an extremely easy thing to do, and let's face it—we're all going to have inefficiencies, we're all going to procrastinate at times, and we're all going to *choose* at times to not do the most effective, nor productive things in business. In fact at least some of the time procrastination and distraction serves a valuable purpose in allowing us to take our foot off the accelerator and have just a few moments rest from the job at hand. Procrastination can also be a way to allow a change of mental stimuli that can help us to use different (subconscious) aspects of our consciousness to passively problem-solve, and/or allow us to more easily enter a 'flow' state when we begin 'working' again. It's a fine line though, and often when we procrastinate we are merely distracting ourselves from the job at hand when the greater gain would be to get it done! This self-sabotaging distraction can be because of a range of self-limiting beliefs and ingrained behaviours related to our feelings of self-worth, achievement and success. Suffice it to say there are many more positive ways to 'actively distract' and to rest than what many of us do. For example instead of allowing distraction by clicking refresh on your social media feed when you're tired, you could have a siesta (which has been shown to improve alertness and cognition) or read, or meditate or do something else truly relaxing…instead of looking at pictures of cats on the internet…

AND there are plenty of things that we can begin to do right now that will help us to get more out of our time, and give us more time to do the things we love (and less of the things we don't. Because distraction and procrastination is one thing…wasting time is another altogether.

Automate Bookings

Automating your booking process is a complete no-brainer as a practitioner. This one, simple action can (at very low cost) free up huge amounts of time for you and make it much easier for your clients to book in a session (difficulty booking is a major reason for failure to book!) It also has another little recognised benefit—it helps to preserve your free time…If you handle all your bookings manually I guarantee that you will make compromises on your time to accommodate clients. This is completely fine at times of course, but I have found that with online booking this issue is completely eliminated. It removes the choice conundrum and people simply book the times that are available…without pushing for a time that's not.

Action: Trial an online booking system

Decide whether you're going to use a booking system (highly recommended)

Research various options. I personally use BookFresh (www.bookfresh.com) which works perfectly for my business and integrates seamlessly with my calendar of choice (Google Calendar).

Tools:

Book Fresh – www.bookfresh.com

Automate Payment

Whether or not you're automating bookings (but again – I stress that you should!) it saves additional time to also automate the client payments. This may seem like a minor detail, but the couple of minutes that it takes to get payment from any client adds up over time. Having automated and pre-payments also removes any awkwardness around asking for payment (a big issue for many practitioners), and also removes the potential for non-payment or late payments that you have to chase up (note: anything that you need to remember and follow up is a time drain!)

Tools such as BookFresh include the option to pay automatically via PayPal and other options.

Accept All Forms of Payment

It may be tempting to not worry about the extra hassle of taking credit and debit cards in your start-up practice but you really want to make it as easy as possible for your clients to pay…and to give them no option BUT to pay! I remember the wise words of my Dad when I first went into business nearly two decades ago; "Accept EVERY form of payment!" What he was basically saying is that a bird in the hand is worth two in the bush…or more appropriately a dollar in your pocket is worth infinitely more than millions in your debtors' ledger!

It is easier than ever to take credit card payments nowadays via PayPal and other services.

Action: Sign up for a payment system

There are a number of options when looking at payment systems for your practice. These range from the most tedious and time-consuming to set up; EFTPOS and credit card facilities in your clinic, through to the most simple; immediate registration payment options such as PayPal. I have used both and at my clinic we have EFTPOS and credit card facilities at reception. For many years now—and especially while travelling around the globe writing and speaking, I have used PayPal as a payment option almost exclusively. The two main reasons for this are: 1) It's simple to set up. With just a few clicks you can be on your way to accepting payments from people via PayPal itself and also through all major credit cards. 2) It integrates seamlessly with almost all booking, events management, shopping cart and web-building software. This in itself is a time and hassle saver that makes the use of PayPal a great option. Some people complain about the fractionally higher payments fees, or the fact that the PayPal site and back-end are not the most easy to use, but in my opinion there isn't much else that gives you the range of benefits with the ease of signup and use that PayPal offers. Other newer options include card readers and associated service providers that attach directly to your smart phone. Check these out and see which option is going to work best for you.

Tools:

PayPal – www.paypal.com

Swipe – www.swpehq.com

Square – www.squareup.com

Automate Information Gathering

My biggest pet peeve when I go to see a practitioner is having to sit down and fill in a paper intake form for all of my data and then wait while they look over it, or have them take all my physical stats and historical data themselves. This is a waste of my time as a patient and it's a massive waste of your time as a practitioner (perhaps THE biggest). Why waste your time writing down general biographical info from your client when this can be completely and seamlessly automated? Your time is worth so much more than that.

A simple and effective solution is to have online forms that your client can fill in and submit at their leisure before the initial consultation. The additional benefit to you and the client is that you're able to peruse these intakes earlier and do additional research before the session. This allows for a better client experience, greater ability for you to deliver results, and a better ability to ask more pertinent follow-on questions within the clinical consultation itself.

Action: Create an online form for your clients to use

There are a range of excellent online form builders available nowadays. When I first entered practice Michael Jordan had just led the Bulls to another 'three-peat', Celine Dion was topping the charts…and there was little in the way of online anything, let alone good third party applications for things like intake forms! How things have changed.

I use the native forms within the Weebly website builder and Wufoo forms almost exclusively. Google forms are also a great option. Remember that if you decide to change platform from Weebly then you will have to recreate your forms, however both Google forms and Wufoo forms are able to be embedded into any site and so you can take those wherever you wind up on the web.

Tools:

Weebly – www.weebly.com

Wufoo – www.wufoo.com

Google forms – www.google.com/google-d-s/createforms.html

Provide as Much Info as Needed to the Client Automatically

The back and forth between client and pracitioner before a sesion is a BIG waste of time and energy for both parties that has no real benefit. If you provide as much detail as possible in your initial email/s to the client (or better yet, within their online booking process) you will save yourself a huge amount of time.

Make sure you provide the following info to your client early in the process:

- Location
- Parking
- What they should bring
- Anything else they need to know

Preview the Client Intake

Do a quick preview of the client intake as soon as you receive it via email. This 'prevision' is *only* to see if there is anything that requires further investigation or research. If additional research is required, either do it immediately (if it will take less than fve minutes as per the '4 Ds'), or if longer is required schedule a time in your diary to do this.

Do another short preview around 20min before your client session to remind yourself of any pertinent aspects of the case.

Automate Your Follow-up Processes
(but still keep it personal!)

Following up clients has to be done…and it takes up time. The problem is that it's easy to forget to follow up, especially if you are really busy, or like me are extremely busy AND are prone to distraction! And it's not because you don't love and care for your clients and patients, it's just that life has a lot of 'stuff' going on. In my clinical experience I have faced two big challenges to improving following up: 1) Automated software solutions take a long time to set up and maintain—completely defeating the purpose of using them, and 2) Manual solutions, like diarising follow-ups, creating spreadsheets and alerts with dates and information to follow up etc. suffer from the same problems—they take a long time to set up and a significant amount of time to maintain.

I have found that as with most things in business (and life) simplifying is the key. Simplify, simplify, simplify!

The simplest solution to a problem is usually the best one!

The simplest way to manage follow ups is to use some freely available basic email add-ons that can completely eliminate the hassles involved with following up. I use FollowUp.cc (www.followup.cc) and Boomerang (www.boomerang.com) for Gmail to automatically return emails to my inbox after a certain period and thereby remind me to follow up with a client. For many of us our inbox serves as a proxy 'to-do' list and so it makes sense that we can use it for reminders and as an integral part of our customer relation strategy.

Example: After the first consultation (within four working days) I send the clients plan via email. I will carbon-copy (CC) this using the Gmail plug-in followup.cc to return to me after four days. When it returns to my inbox four days later, it reminds me to ask the client how they're getting on starting into the plan. I will then 'boomerang' this or any reply from the client for one week later, and then two weeks and then one month, and so on. With this strategy I'm able to stay in contact regularly but more and more infrequently as the client integrates patterns of behaviour and needs less support from me.

Note: As compared to many productivity 'gurus' I don't recommend using completely automated (in other words pre-written) emails at regularly scheduled intervals because I am in the business of working with people personally, and am providing a service not a product. In personal emails we can interact with the client more effectively, making reference to their consultation, their health challenges and their plan, which we'd be unable to do via a generic email.

Action: Set up and start using FollowUp.cc and/or Boomerang immediately

- Find the plug-in for Boomerang if you use Gmail. Install the plug-in and begin to use it by testing 'boomeranging' a few messages for a set time in the future. Remember that you can set custom times too

(some of my favourites are 9am Monday and 9am Wednesday)

- Sign up for FollowUp.cc. The free version works perfectly well for most practitioners (particularly if you use Boomerang as well). Send a couple of test emails with a follow up time CC'ed in to become used to using the tool.

Tools:

Boomerang – www.boomeranggmail.com/
FollowUp.cc – www.followup.cc

Acquiring customers and taking bookings and payments is only half the battle won. The rest revolves around continuing to meet the needs of those clients, and in continuing to have the efficiencies in your business that allow positive cash-flow and positive 'time-flow'.

There are a number of time effectiveness techniques that serve the dual goals of increasing your available time and allowing more effective, ongoing customer engagement.

Use a Good Online Calendar

Putting aside 'blocks' of time is imperative for making the best use of our time (multi-tasking and doing things 'on-the-fly' sucks!) And a good calendar is essential to being able to do this. You can stay on track by blocking aside time for all the important things in your life (like seeing clients, writing, surfing and Jiu Jitsu!), all the tasks that must be completed in your business, and to send reminders of these to your many devices, as well as to have a visual representation of your working week. I really wouldn't be able to function well without a good to-do list and a great online calendar.

You could simply use the calendar within your online booking system, or preferably, a cross-platform calendar that syncs with your booking system. I like Google calendar because it syncs with most major online booking systems, other calendars and is ubiquitous across all devices.

Action: Start using an online calendar.

1. Choose an online calendar (I suggest using Google calendar)
2. Sync this with your online booking system
3. Set up all your regularly occuring appointments

Tools:

Google calendar – www.google.com/calendar

CHAPTER NINE

Making Sure

Keeping your business on track

"SUSTAINABILITY CAN'T BE LIKE SOME SORT OF A MORAL SACRIFICE OR POLITICAL DILEMMA OR A PHILANTHROPICAL CAUSE. IT HAS TO BE A DESIGN CHALLENGE."

~ BJARKE INGELS

Maintaining your business and all the inertia that you've built up involves keeping on top of some of the mundane compliance 'stuff' (like taxes...) and also periodic check-ins and reviews of how well you're doing and whether you are still in-line with your ethos and values (in other words: are you still loving this and being inspired by it?)

Stay Engaged with Your Client Base

Remaining in contact with your client base is imperative for building community and for staying 'front of mind'.

Blog posts, articles and even social media are relatively passive, whereas direct communication, be it a phone call or a newsletter compels someone to more action.

Think of it this way: if you post to Facebook it will either be noticed or not, and in any event it will simply move down someone's feed until it is no longer visible and thereby no longer relevant. However an email requires someone to actually look at it (even if just the headline) and perform an action (even if that action is to hit 'delete').

If I had my time in practice all over again I would be much better at keeping consistent customer databases and using them for direct contact in the form of informational newsletters. Several years ago, with the rise of social media, I let many of my databases fall into redundancy, and it wasn't until tech entrepreneur Julien Emery asked me about my direct campaign strategy that I realized I no longer had one! It was then that I reevaluated using email lists and campaigns again.

Nowadays there are a number of excellent third-party email newsletter software providers. They all offer the ability to create template newsletters with a rich array of features including web and social media integration, embeddable sign-up widgets for social media and your website and auto-unsubscribe so that you are sure not to spam anyone.

I've used a range of these including: Constant Contact, AWeber and MailChimp.

I can highly recommend both AWeber and MailChimp, although for many practitioners MailChimp is the better option due to it being free for anything up to 2000 subscribers.

Action: Start a newsletter list immediately

Whether you start to use it immediately or not, start a newsletter database to capture interested peoples details and give you the ability to email information, events and news to them.

1. Go to a web based email newsletter provider such as MailChimp.
2. Sign up and enter your company information
3. Set up your first list
4. Copy the embed codes for the 'sign-up' widget and embed in your website and social media

Tools:

MailChimp – www.mailchimp.com

AWeber – www.aweber.com

Constant Contact – www.constantcontact.com

Continually Clarify Your Business Purpose

It is critical for the Time Rich Practitioner to stay on purpose. This requires taking the time to periodically 'check-in' and make sure that you are doing what you love, and not being distracted by 'lower gain' activities. These lower gain activities are not necessarily things that don't pay so well, they are more likely activities that you get drawn into (do you have a problem saying no too?!) and that aren't all that enjoyable. Doing things in life that are unenjoyable is inevitable…but hey, if you don't have to do something AND if it's distracting you from the truly important work of being an awesome practitioner should you really be doing it?

Action: Reassess whether you're working 'on-purpose'

1. Take a few minutes to sit down and think about your last few days and weeks of practice.

2. Ask yourself the simple question "Am I on purpose?"

3. Try to answer this question intuitively and immediately.

4. If the answer is Yes, good work. If No, then think of why this might be.

5. Go back and take a look at your *values determination* sheet and remind yourself of your most important core value points.

6. Which 'low gain' activities are drawing you from purpose?

7. Make a plan to reduce or eliminate (use the '4 Ds') low gain activities to bring you back into line with your passion and purpose in practice.

I describe the practice of 'self-audits' in *Choosing You*. These are mini, daily audits that you perform at the end of your day to see whether you really lived the way you wanted to, and to use the times when you didn't as a chance to learn and grow. This personal audit can be easily translated, and is a valuable practice for business too.

Daily Revisions and Reviews

A valuable daily practice is to review and revise your day. By reviewing your day, from start to finish, you can mindfully see how you acted and identify the times when you acted in a way that you're not happy with. By doing this you can learn from your actions in order to change them.

In going through these revisions and reviews we can also congratulate ourselves for taking actions that are positive and that are feeding into personal growth.

I find it best to do this review at the end of the working day rather than at the very end of the day. This provides a 'book-end' to the day and allows for you to then relax without any work commitments and wind down.

Action: Revise and review your day

- At the end of your working day (or any other time that suits your schedule) put aside 10 or 15 minutes to be alone and look back over your day (the last 24 hours).

- Turn off your phone, computer etc. and don't allow other things to distract you. Find a comfortable place and either lie or sit down or get into any other position that is comfortable and conducive to visualisation.

- Close your eyes, take a few deep breaths in and out through your nose and starting with when you first woke up, walk yourself through the day-that-was. Visualise the events that happened – what you did, who you met, how you acted in situations and reacted to events. As you go through you will notice things you did well, and also things that you are not happy with because they are not conducive to achieving your goals. If need be take a few notes. If something was counterproductive to goals you have set and to visualisations you have been making, jot it down somewhere you won't lose it (your journal is the best place for this) and make a mental note.

As a result of what you have reviewed in your day you will probably have some subjects for positive reinforcement and visualisation. Write down subjects for visualisation and any notes you may have about how you could act differently (more positively—and for a better result) in certain situations. Usually a few key words or phrases suffice.

When we have been mindful of how we act, when we have goals and dreams about who we want to be, and when we take the time to review our actions we can see some of our real character traits – some of which we might dislike. Always remember that the way you act is as a result of conditioning since even before you were born….BUT you have the power to change it.

Watching the Books

A tip that I took from Gordon Ramsey's book *Playing with Fire* was to make sure to have a good accounting system, and to set up your systems for monitoring your cash flow, expenses and to stay compliant (especially with tax!) from the very beginning of your business. Many practitioners I have coached wait until they have grown, taken on staff and started pulling in decent revenue before looking at this area, but this often creates a time consuming and stress inducing period in which you try to create accounts out of nothing and deal with unpaid taxes. Not to mention that having no real understanding of what the cashflow situation is in your business is potentially calamitous!

With online, cloud-based and highly automated software systems now available there is no need to wait. Even if you can't afford an accountant the least you can do is to sign up for an online solution like Xero at the cost of around 10 bucks a week and sit down to do your reconciliations periodically.

Doing your taxes and accounts is a big, scary proposition for people but really it need not be. I actually do my taxes and accounts myself (even though I'm fond of outsourcing almost everything else!)

I simply set aside one morning, once per month to take care of all tax, accounts and compliance matters in my businesses. Usually with the help of Xero I am able to get this all done in under two hours.

Actions: Sort out your accounting process

- Set up a timeline for doing your business compliance
- Find the tool that works for you (I highly recommend Xero)

Tools:

Xero – www.xero.com

Note: Always make sure that all your business expenditure only goes through your bank account and perhaps a credit card. Try not to make cash purchases as the hassle of keeping track of them and putting them into the set of accounts in my opinion simply isn't worth it.

CHAPTER TEN

Making it More

Leveraging for greater time and cash flow

"YOU HAVE LIMITED TIME TO SELL, BUT YOU CAN SELL AN INFINITE AMOUNT OF PRODUCT..."
~ MAURICE HARVEY (MY DAD)

No matter how successful we are at creating a viable and sought-after service, we will eventually near our available time and price-offering ceiling. This means that there will inevitably come a point at which we can't, or aren't prepared to: a) do any more work and b) charge any more for our service offering.

It's easy to see that the time we spend doing what we love is limited by our energy levels and other time commitments, and so if we need to provide more revenue/profit to do some of the things we want to do in life, simply working more and more is a very self-limiting way to approach this. Many people may say (somewhat justifiably) that 'you can always charge more' but there are many reasons why we may not be prepared to do this. One reason is that there are certain 'tipping' points at which our services are simply priced out of the market. While we may be able to charge very large amounts in comparison to others in the industry, there will come a point for all of us at which there will be an exponential drop off in clientele, based on what we are charging and this will outweigh the increased revenue per client. This point occurs when the amount we charge is deemed by a significant amount of our potential customers to be greater than the perceived value of what they are going to receive.

There are of course ways to add value, and we can become such respected experts that the ceiling is indeed very high, but inevitably that tipping point will come to all of us at some stage.

Perhaps a more important reason for not being able to increase prices for our services is that we are not willing to do so. We may be reluctant to increase our prices when those that we would like to help can no longer afford our services. If we get to a point at which only the very wealthy are able to afford to see us, this may not serve one or more of the philanthropic and moral goals that we have set as being important to what we do. This is one of the primary reasons that in spite of being very busy I continue to charge what I charge. It is a high rate in comparison to the industry, but still one that I have found that a large proportion of people are still able to budget for and afford.

You can however increase your earning potential in ways other than simply raising prices ad infinitum.

Using the Power of Referral and Product to Increase Earnings

Selling Product

Selling product as a practitioner is a contentious issue. It is a logical extension of your business that will increase revenue and profitability. However we need to be very aware of our ethical duty of care for our clients and patients, and this includes not becoming a shill for the supplement companies, nor selling anything to a client that isn't going to give a great (health or performance) return on their investment.

It is important to ask several questions of yourself when deciding whether to prescribe a nutritional or herbal supplement or sell any other product to a client or patient:

- *Is the product congruent with your values and ethos?*
- *Is the product otherwise of good quality?*
- *Is the product sustainable in a pragmatic fashion?*
- *Most importantly – is the product going to be of benefit to your client and is their return on investment for this product likely to be justified?*

If the answer to any of the above is no, *you cannot sell that product, or sell it to that customer or patient.*

Several other mitigating factors should also be considered in your choice to prescribe or not.

Confirmation bias

When your only tool is a hammer every problem appears to be a nail…When we have a product that we use, recommend and even dare I say love…it can be easy to see it fitting in to everyone's plan, when an objective eye would be a little more circumspect. Be aware of your potential confirmation biases!

Green allopathy

The term 'green allopathy' is one that describes the system employed by many naturopaths and nutritionists in which they treat symptoms with supplements, herbs or other modality remedies. Notwithstanding that I don't believe this is even what naturopathy or clinical nutrition should be, it can also lead to over-prescription and this can (even if sub-consciously) be driven by a commercial imperative. It absolutely grinds my gears when I see someone walking out of a naturopath's office with hundreds (and sometimes thousands) of dollars' worth of pills and potions when simple dietary and lifestyle interventions could have provided a more credible, cost-effective solution. Please don't do this!

Action: Become critically aware of confirmation bias and symptom based prescription.

1. Take the files from your last ten clients and look at what you prescribed for them.

2. Ask yourself the following questions: Will the client get appreciable benefit from that supplement (or product)? Could they have gotten similar benefits from another intervention? Could I have done anything differently to provide better benefits at a similar or cheaper cost to the client?

3. This need not be an exhaustive exercise, but is simply a good way to remain mindful of how you could serve your clients better without falling into the dual traps of confirmation bias and green allopathy.

Bottom line: There's nothing wrong with selling product to your clients. I do it…I even create products and am a stakeholder in several supplement companies. But it's got to be the right product, for the right client, and for you.

Referring Product

With the same caveats as above, referring clients to products can be an even better approach for practitioners. Holding stock, having to (potentially) pay for the product before it's sold, and the inevitable headaches of inventory control and forecasting are not always a good fit for practitioners who would rather be focussed on servicing their clients, and it can be more hassle than it's worth. Many systems exist for practitioners to refer sales to distributors, wholesalers and retail outlets and get a commission for doing so. Often the companies will also provide a very healthy discount to your client. Win-win.

Action: Determine which products you can refer to clients
(Note: This is not a cynical exercise in trying to sell more to clients, it is an exercise in determining what you already refer and how you can gain a small return from this AND enable your clients to also receive a discount.)

1. Make a list of all the items you currently recommend to clients, or would recommend to the majority of your clients.
2. Ask yourself: "Do I currently sell these or refer to an incentivised program? Or do I simply tell them what to get and they get it from someone else?"

If you refer customers to other outlets without remuneration then it's in your best interest to find the suppliers, distributors or practitioner portals that allow you to be remunerated effectively, or approach the outlet that you currently refer to and discuss creating a referral remuneration program. This can be incredibly effective. A great system that I have used in the past is to have a practitioner prescription pad for supplements and herbs that has the address and details of a (local) dispensary and all your details on too (like a Doctor's prescription pad). Write your prescription on the pad and then the client can take this to the store to buy their products. The store knows that you have sent them in and is able to remunerate you according to the agreement you have put in place.

Tools:

NuZest Professional Partner program – www.nuzest.co.nz
Pacific Health – www.pachealth.co.nz

Affiliate Sales

Affiliate sales are basically referrals and could fit into the category above, but I wanted to differentiate between core products that you are more likely to hold stock of (albeit in possibly small amounts) and either buy at a wholesale rate or refer, and retailers who simply offer commissions for online referrals. These are often big companies like Amazon that offer a large variety of products and have robust affiliate systems.

For example, in addition to supplements and herbal medicines I recommend a lot of books, e-books and audio books to my clients to help them to achieve their goals. I would recommend the books anyway, and I don't mind where they get them from, but I provide links to Amazon (or in the case of audio-books to Audible) in their plans to make their life easier (otherwise I'd probably get a call asking where they could purchase the book anyway!)

It simply makes sense that this link should be an affiliate link from which I get a commission—rather than a simple link from which I get no additional benefit. There is no difference from the clients point of view (they get the same price and can choose whether or not to purchase and read the book) but for me it's the difference between getting a couple of extra dollars, and not, and believe me, for my business several dollars coming from a variety of sources adds up to a significant add-on revenue stream.

Action: Determine what can you refer right now?

- Make a list of all the 'other' products that you recommend to people.
- Do affiliate systems exist for these?

Tools:

Amazon affiliates – www.amazon.com

Audible affiliates – www.audible.com

Sponsorships

This is a somewhat minor consideration, but if you are (or are becoming) a key opinion leader (KOL) in your field, companies may want to give you free or discounted stuff!

As with the other points in this chapter you should only ever align with companies with which you have a shared value and ethos set, and that you would otherwise recommend. But if those things are true, then if someone wants to give you something that you'd otherwise buy anyway… you'd be mad not to take it!

It may seem an inconsequential factor, but there are many succesful practitioners involved in blogging, writing and speaking that derive a large amount of their relative income 'in kind' from companies providing them products. I vividly remember in my days as a competitive athlete saving many thousands of dollars a year as a result of being sponsored for shoes, apparel and nutritional supplements.

Create Informational Products

Informational products provide an additional way to achieve a highly leveraged, ongoing income stream. Books (like the one you are reading), audiobooks and e-books are all products that don't need to be held as stock items and that can be sold remotely by a third party and without you having to handle any aspect of logistics and supply.

Live the Shit Out of Your Practice Life!

"YOU HAVE YOUR BRUSH, YOU HAVE YOUR COLOURS, YOU PAINT PARADISE, THEN IN YOU GO."

~ NIKOS KAZANTZAKIS

(FROM *ZORBA THE GREEK)*

Passion and purpose are the dual edges to the sword of living a life that is truly worth living.

Sometimes the sham and drudgery of the 'stuff' that we have to do, or feel otherwise compelled to do, can seem to take the 'edge' off that sword of passion and purpose. And that's why I wrote this book—to try and make the process of doing 'the work' just that little bit easier. In doing so we can retain more of that passion and purpose and give back to others, our family and friends and to ourselves.

A question I have paraphrased from *Time Rich Cash Optional: an unconventional guide to happiness:*

Because let's face it – it's easy to be alive. Alive is the default. You didn't need to do much to wake up this morning...

And it's equally true that for almost all of us, almost all of the time we need to work and we need to earn. I am under no illusions about the realities of life. BUT we can choose to do something we love, and in doing so we need not compromise on having the money and the time to live a safe, comfortable, joy filled existence.

To do this though takes the courage to choose to do it and to accept that you may have to step outside the norm and live by your own set of rules. And once the choice is made you need to keep on doing the work, doing it well, and most importantly doing it with love and with passion.

So what are you waiting for?

Let's do this thing!

SELECTED BIBLIOGRAPHY & RECOMMENDED READING

Allen, David. 2002, *Getting Things Done*, Penguin, New York.

Aristotle, Revised Edition, 2009, *The Nicomachean Ethics, Oxford World Classics*, Oxford University Press, New York.

Beilecki, Tessa. *Wild at Heart*. Audio book read by author. Louisville, CO: Sounds True, 2006

Bond, Michael. *The Pursuit of Happiness*. New Scientist. 4 Oct. 2003.
<http://www.newscientist.com/article/mg18024155.100-the-pursuit-of-happiness.html>

Cameron, Julia. 1992, *The Artists Way*, Tarcher, New York

Das, Surya, 2000, *Awakening to the Sacred*, Three Rivers Press, New York.

Doidge, Norman. 2007 *The Brain that Changes Itself*, Penguin, New York.

Ferriss, Timothy. 2007, *The 4 Hour Workweek,* Crown Archetype, New York.

Godin, Seth. *Linchpin.* Audio book read by author. New York: Random House Audio, 2010

Harvey, Cliff. 2009, *Choosing You! How you can choose to live the life of your dreams … RIGHT NOW!,* CC Publishing, Auckland. New Zealand

Harvey, Cliff. 2011, *Tiime Rich Cash Optional: an unconventional guide to happiness.* CC Publishing, Auckland. New Zealand.

Harvey, Cliff. *Stop Getting Through.* <u>Cliffdog.com</u> 23 Feb. 2010. <http://cliffdog.blogspot.com/2010/02/stop-getting-through.html>

Kelly, Kevin. *1,000 True Fans.* <u>The Technium </u>March 2008. <http://www.kk.org/thetechnium/archives/2008/03/1000_true_fans.php>

Lipton, Bruce, 2008, *The Biology of Belief,* Hay House, New York.

Marquez, Gabriel Garcia. 2003 *Living to Tell the Tale,* Knopf, New York.

Pert, Candace, 1999, *Molecules of Emotion,* Simon & Schuster, Chicago.

Pinchot, Gifford. *The Gift Economy.* <u>Pinchot & Company</u> n.d.
<http://company.pinchot.com/MainPages/BooksArticl es/OtherArticles/GiftEconomy.html>

Ramsay, Gordon. (2008). *Gordon Ramsay's playing with fire.* HarperCollins UK.

Thich Nhat Hanh, 1994, *The Miracle of Mindfulness,* Beacon Press, Boston.

USEFUL WEBSITES & ONLINE READING

About Cliff

www.cliffharvey.com

www.cliffdog.com

Businesses by Cliff

www.holisticperformancenutrition.com

www.nuzest.com

Chapter 1.

'Start With Why' by Simon Sinek – www.startwithwhy.com

Chapter 2.

Dreamline Worksheet –
http://www.technotheory.com/download/DreamlineWorkshe
et2.0.xls

Book Recommendations –
www.holisticperformancenutrition.com/recommended-
books.html

Chapter 4.

Website Builders

Weebly – www.weebly.com

Wix – www.wix.com

Squarespace – www.squarespace.com

Training Tilt – www.trainingtilt.com

iStock Photo: Royalty-free Images – www.istockphoto.com

Chapter 5.

Blogging Platforms

Wordpress – www.wordpress.com / www.wordpress.org

Blogger – www.blogspot.com

Typepad – www.typepad.com

Website Rankings

Alexa - www.alexa.com

Social and Online Presence

About Me – www.about.me

Facebook – www.facebook.com

Twitter – www.twitter.com

Instagram – www.instagram.com

Pinterest – www.pinterest.com

YouTube - www.youtube.com

Creating Content Alerts

Google Scholar – www.scholar.google.com

Google alerts (standard) – www.google.com/alerts

Google Forms – www.google.com/google-d-s/createforms.html

Email Productivity Tools

Followup.CC – www.followup.cc

Boomerang for Gmail – www.boomerang.com

Calendar Software

Google Calendar - www.google.com/calendar

Chapter 9.

Email Newsletter and Database Software

Mail Chimp – www.mailchimp.com

AWeber – www.aweber.com

Constant Contact – www.constantcontact.com

Cloud Based Accounting Software

Xero – www.xero.com

Chapter 10.

Affiliate Programs

NuZest NZ – www.nuzest.co.nz

Pacific Health – www.pachealth.co.nz

Amazon Affiliates – www.amazon.com

Audible Affiliates – www.audible.com

CLIFF HARVEY is a clinician, researcher, academic, and serial health and wellness entrepreneur. Since 1998 he has been  helping people to live healthier, happier lives through his clinical nutrition and naturopathic medicine practice, and books, lectures and workshops.

His books *Choosing You!* and the Ashton Wylie Book Award finalist *Time Rich Cash Optional: an unconventional guide to happiness* are inspired by his remarkable life-journey, which has included recovering from the effects of Crohn's Disease to win two world championships in All-Round Weightlifting, working with elite level athletes and founding several successful health and wellness businesses.

Cliff is the founder of Holistic Performance Nutrition™ an organisation providing graduate level education for nutrition, fitness and natural health practitioners and those passionate about nutrition and health.

www.hpn.ac.nz

www.cliffharvey.com

www.ingramcontent.com/pod-product-compliance
Lightning Source LLC
Chambersburg PA
CBHW050951050726
47592CB00007B/2524